Prayers of Encouragement

Chosen and illustrated
by Chris Coe

kevin
mayhew

This beautifully illustrated collection of prayers, poems and Bible readings offers words of encouragement to uplift and bring hope.

As you read, remember that God promises to be with us always, in every circumstance of life, and in times of need he draws especially close to us.

Look to God, for he promises to care and protect, strengthen and heal, bless and guide. He is our faithful shepherd, companion and friend.

The Lord's Prayer

Our Father who art in heaven,
hallowed be thy name.
Thy kingdom come,
thy will be done,
on earth as it is in heaven.
Give us this day our daily bread;
and forgive us our trespasses,
as we forgive those
who trespass against us.
And lead us not into temptation
but deliver us from evil.
For thine is the kingdom,
the power and the glory,
for ever and ever.
Amen.

The blessing of the Lord be upon you

Psalm 129:8

My presence will go with you
and I will give you rest

Exodus 33:14

A Blessing

May the Lord bless you
and take care of you.

May the Lord be kind
and gracious to you.

May the Lord look on you with favour
and give you peace.

Numbers 6:24-26

Footprints

One night I dreamed
I was walking along the beach with the Lord.
Many scenes from my life flashed across the sky.
In each scene I noticed footprints in the sand.
Sometimes there were two sets of footprints,
other times there was one set of footprints.
This bothered me because I noticed
that during the low periods of my life,
when I was suffering from
anguish, sorrow or defeat,
I could see only one set of footprints.

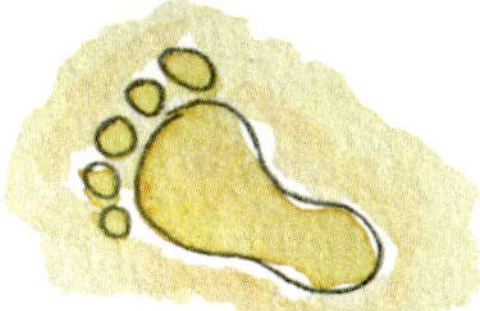

So I said to the Lord,
'You promised me, Lord,
that if I followed you,
you would walk with me always.
But I have noticed that during
the most trying periods of my life
there has only been one
set of footprints in the sand.
Why, when I needed you most,
have you not been there for me?'

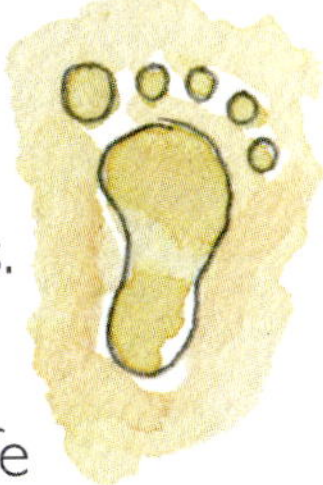

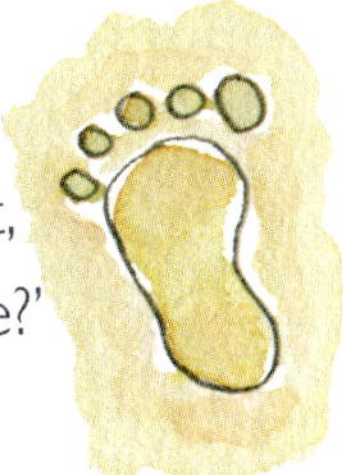

The Lord replied,
'The times when you have seen only one set
of footprints, my child, is when I carried you.'

Mary Stevenson (1922–1999)

The eternal God is your refuge

Deuteronomy 33:27

When Dreams Are Broken

When dreams are broken things
and joy has fled,
there is Jesus.

When hope is a struggle
and faith a fragile thread,
there is Jesus.

When grief is a shadow
and peace unknown,
there is Jesus.

When we need the assurance
that we're not alone,
there is Jesus.

When I find it hard to pray,
troubles seeming here to stay;
dreams in ruins, turned to dust,
sorrow undermining trust,
Lord, be with me, by my side,
be my help, my strength, my guide.
Lead me onwards by your grace,
till I meet you, face to face.

Nick Fawcett

The Lord is good, a stronghold in the day of trouble

Nahum 1:7

He has given us great and precious promises

2 Peter 1:4

An Everyday Prayer

Lord, in all I do today,
remind me that
there's just one way
to do things
that I do best,
to put my mind
and heart at rest.
And that's to put
in your great hands,
my life, that you alone
have planned.

God Is the Answer

He comes as a Companion
to the lonely,
a Faithful Friend
who cares and understands.

He comes as a Physician
to the hurting,
with tenderness
and healing in his hands.

He comes as a Protector
to the helpless,
a Shepherd who calls

all his lambs by name,
a Father who sees

every child as special,
whose gentle heart
loves each of us the same.

He comes, the Consolation
of the suffering,
the Light that breaks
through darkness and despair.
He comes, and we discover
that his presence
is the loving answer to
our every prayer.

I know the plans I have for you, says the Lord

Jeremiah 29:11

Be at Peace

Do not look forward
to what might happen tomorrow;
the same everlasting Father
who cares for you today
will take care of you tomorrow
and every day.

Either he will shield you
from suffering
or he will give you
unfailing strength to bear it.

Be at peace, then,
and put aside all
anxious thoughts and imaginings.

The Cross in My Pocket

I carry a cross in my pocket,
a simple reminder to me
of the fact that I am a Christian,
no matter where I may be.
This little cross is not magic,
nor is it a good luck charm,
it isn't meant to protect me
from every physical harm.
It's not for identification
for all the world to see,
it's simply an understanding
between my Saviour and me.

When I put my hand in my pocket
to bring out a coin or key,
the cross is there to remind me
of the price he paid for me.
It reminds me, too, to be thankful
for my blessings day by day
and strive to serve him better
in all that I do and say.
It's also a daily reminder
of the peace and comfort I share
with all who know my master
and give themselves to his care.

So I carry a cross in my pocket,
reminding no one but me
that Jesus Christ is Lord of my life
if only I'll let him be.

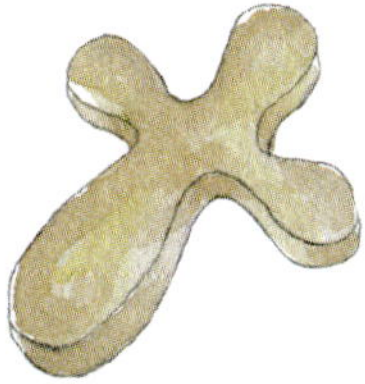

Verna Mae Thomas

God has poured out his love into our hearts

Romans 5:5

When you're lonely,
I wish you love.

When you're down,
I wish you joy.

When you're troubled,
I wish you peace.

When things are complicated,
I wish you simple beauty.

When things look empty,
I wish you hope.

Wings of Faith

Give us, Lord, a special faith,
unlimited and free,
a faith that isn't bound
by what we know or what we see.

A faith that trusts the sunshine
even when there is no light,
a faith that hears the morning song's
soft echo in the night.

A faith that somehow rises
past unhappiness or pain,
knowing that in every loss
your goodness will remain.

A faith that finds your steadfast love
sufficient for all things,
a faith that lifts the heart above
and gives the spirit wings.

To everything there is a season,
and a time for every activity under heaven

Ecclesiastes 3:1

Be still and know that I am God

Psalm 46:10

The Peace of God

Do not worry about anything,
but in everything,
by prayer and supplication
with thanksgiving let your requests
be made known to God.

And the peace of God,
which surpasses all understanding,
will guard your hearts and your minds
in Christ Jesus.

Philippians 4:6,7

The 23rd Psalm

The Lord is my shepherd,
I shall not be in want.
He makes me lie down
in green pastures,
he leads me beside quiet waters,
he restores my soul.
He guides me in paths of righteousness
for his name's sake.
Even though I walk through
the valley of the shadow of death,
I will fear no evil,
for you are with me;
your rod and your staff,
they comfort me.

You prepare a table before me
in the presence of my enemies.
You anoint my head with oil;
my cup overflows.
Surely goodness and love
will follow me
all the days of my life,
and I will dwell
in the house of the Lord
for ever.

The Lord will go with you. He will not forget you

Deuteronomy 31:6

God grant me the serenity
to accept the things
I cannot change,
the courage to change
the things I can,
and the wisdom to know
the difference.

KEVIN MAYHEW LTD
Buxhall, Stowmarket, Suffolk, IP14 3BW
E-mail: info@kevinmayhewltd.com
Website: www.kevinmayhew.com

9 8 7 6 5 4 3 2 1 0

ISBN 978 1 84867 522 3
Catalogue No. 1501354

Design and illustrations by Chris Coe

Printed and bound in China